Published by Augur Editions
Santa Ana, California

Library of Congress Control Number: 2021906650

ISBN: 978-0-578-87177-6

Printed in the United States of America

C O N T E N T S

NAMELESS

A   D   R   I   F   T

it scares me how

the wind and I

both readily change direction

and how nobody

that I know

has really felt me go

A   PARADOX   OF   LOSTNESS

the crisp dawn

of my unyielding horizon

evades me,

like blooming dust

in warm wet light

unruly, intangible

and always out of reach,

I breathe in my fate-

and the echoes of

my own foot guide me

I am my own religion

called on by fickle

mistress of mine

divine inspirations

insanity,

by any other name,

I pray to the foes

of my own becoming

and the world

spitteth back at me

the sincerities

of my pleas

I CALL MY NAME AND THEN I HIDE

my baby is crowned

in a wide blue sky.

can love, with such certainty

change, or move, or die?

sister,

you don't make it out alive

crying on the curbside,

I left you there to lie

reaching out to grasp for greatness

eyes closed wide

I am cursive in the street,

I laugh loudly while I cry

does it hurt to change?

I call my name and then I hide

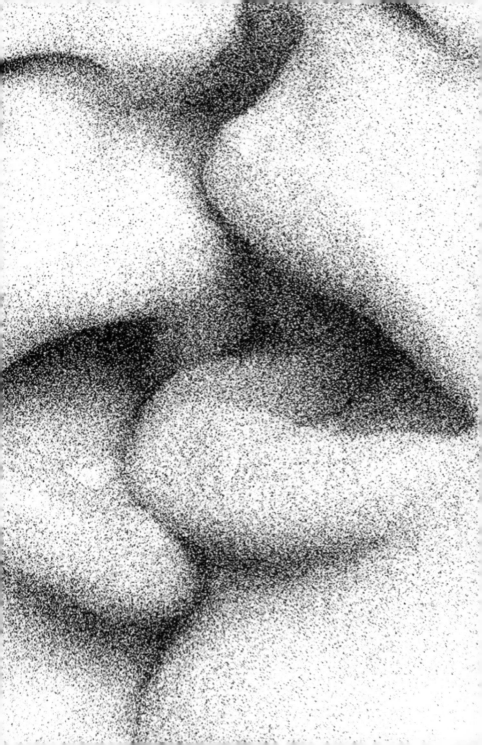

PRAYERS   FOR   BECOMING

that unattainable knowing-

the sweet comfort

of undeniable selfhood

that belongs to

no woman nor man,

nor I

escape me

they who seek themself

find inward answers

of unwritten delusions-

and questions forged

in mirrors and time

this path, led on

by iterations

that I will follow

blindly and to

my own demise,

bears greatness

birthed by wisdom

and certainty

in uncertain ties

GROWN   TOO   TALL

dysphoria swings,

heavy and low-

barren and fruitless

weightless,

I'm empty.

Is This Growth?

on the days I cannot

see my feet upon ground,

or feel myself as solid,

I see I am not

who I thought

in the story

of things as they were

to come,

and to be

I will do all I can-

influence need comfort,

and unique experiences

were forever my outlook.

thrust long and diligently.

I came-

righteous, fallen

shining and bitter

I did not want-

and I am aware, now

that I am not

the same

TONGUE PRESSED HOT AGAINST DESTINY

beauty in no namesake

is mythical to Me,

like holiness sat in stone

or cloudy unknowns

who command none

but prayer and unkept virtue

taken form in abandoned gods

are Mine unwritten idealisms-

exceptionalisms

with halos bruised, but bright

that I roll in undue mud

are you getting my signal?

I speak in tongues

of meaninglessness

that I confess

lives as grand and shaking

as my own heaven's fall

inspired hand, keep off

commencement of my being-

with invocations from silence

and my twisted reliance

on magic and sweet delusions, bulging

wishes as big as fists

I give up prayers to all that hear

the aching of true lies;

is it not what you dream of,

when divinity's more likely speak

with heady and holy intuition, slaked?

hark on harking

doses on my tongue,

like little hail marys, I slip

akin wide eyed big sky'd worship

to rockaby mine lines to shape,

starting with my border

fruition comes late but most bearing,

under burdens of hideousness

and death caught blindly,

I speak to highness, kindly-

my mother, my father, my spirit, my son

this is my body, and this is my blood

at the swift resurrection

and immediating dismemberment

of my reassurance-

I pay the penance,

with my tongue pressed hot

against destiny

EVER   FLOWING,   I   FEEL   YOU

I follow,

blindly

down dead end streets

and dimly-lit gutters,

twinkling in moon light

boats afloat dry land

under free and whirring noises

like blasts of wind

that speak no name

wandering through

heavy summer air

and my minefields

of stunted expectations,

I think about calling your name

and my body aches in step

with cracking bones

and blindness-

met by purpose or incapable sight,

always smells sweeter

than the darkness blooms

led on by assumed responsibility

and insufficient endings,

possibilities mist sharply

and more similar to grief

from ugly beginnings

and dashed hopes

of things that could,

pointed brightnesses

are rare and unheard-

yet still I seek them

desperately

under artificial glows

that turn my shadow long,

pores swell exceptionally

and ugly growth

sprawls before me

ducking madness

and things that stick,

elasticity, discarded-

snaps more quickly

than relief can stretch

and on I walk,

stirring and worn

A   NEW   KIND   OF   SPRING

sometimes, I remember his name

and how I used to say it

like I was scared of it's beauty

at the top of the world,

I collapsed in daisies and naivety-

scraped both my knees

when my vision went bleary

left to sat by you

in a puddle of this belief

that love could be true or honest,

I trusted, too

quickly for a boy so bruised

I almost ran straight up

to heaven, bursting in

my closet contrail temperament,

all steam and exploding regret

from that same new pain

and it's ever-still

surprising ceaselessness

my heart broke a few same ways

on that first day of spring,

like how some scabs don't heal

but split and bloom,

bloody in familiarity-

a permanently inked

needled symphony

of insecurity, hand-held

in the obscurity

of truth laid bare in impurity

I   WASH   MY   HANDS   IN   MUD

I lost myself-

in that

heavy, bouncing tune

I felt him go left,

and his heart

went with him too

speeding car on down the 5

skirting white lines and goodbyes

from here to compton, flew.

pancakes on the concrete floor-

ruins of my home

destiny that doesn't stick

I do, I do, I do

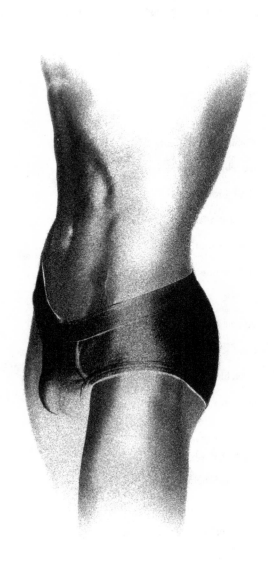

FAMILIAR   RUNS   IN   MY   FABRIC

if I was a color

today, I am sand.

as shifting as I am many-

the reluctance

of my brokenness

is worn in fashion

with the beating

and the unbound

do you scare yourself,

like I scare me?

stretching in the realm

of what's not real to see,

I keep the edges of myself

sketched, lightly

like I am fragile like I am strong

impassioned like I am a fraud

changing faces with

the certainty of

a brand new god

don't speak my name-

I don't like the sound

it never belonged to me,

it's all theirs somehow

I know that I'm blind

and I sing without sound

all the lines that make me

feel used, and now

my corners are alight again

with all that golden now

EAT ME, DRINK ME, SPIT ME OUT

eat me, drink me, spit me out

dark, sweaty, and unflinching

> you don't look human,
>
> you don't look like a person

I ask him what he means, with a wary smile-

he sees the fear in my eyes,

and tells me it's a compliment

> pretty like a girl.
>
> handsome like a boy.
>
> you don't look real.

he licks my face-

and I feel his saliva

sink into my pores

I don't feel real, either

staring at the ceiling,

hands pull on me-

and I feel his shirt,

wet with sweat

panting.

dick against my thigh.

tepid breath.

I don't recognize me;

lying as still as I can.

like I am a doll,

with hard and plastic skin.

he tells me I can go-

destruction,

I vomit bliss

CONVICTED   BRUISING

swollen with possibility

that leaves a bitter taste

like an end I stand-

mirrored,

the distance from myself

feels further

I fall back to my knees,

the earth moves once more

and alarms scream,

shaking, and bloody.

begging for relief,

silence again returns my call.

decided and grasping,

arms hold me and then let me go

SPLIT   ENDS

moving quickly and

without direction,

I am in the ashes

breathe lightning-

drifting lungs

fill comfortably

through colored smoke

and war torn laughter

I escape the night-

in the new breeze,

darkness tastes like freedom

and numbness feels like home

under false hope

and that same

crumbling dream-we all stand

and then cheer

and then scream

FEVER   DREAM

glowing

in the light of new love,

lightning colors and shaking sounds-

he asked if I was happy

dumb and smiling,

bouncing blind eyes look in me,

and mad laugh escape my throat

tilted and widened,

a smile jump upon my lip-

and I turn, to turn to go

standing in the outline

of fundamental truths,

I feel your warmth leave

A   FRUITFUL   SEASON

I spent the summer

in the arms of strange men

distractions with strong faces

and names

that I drink from

when I can't remember my own

skin tickled pink,

I peel the flaking pieces

of myself back, slowly

lying next to muscles

and warm bones

who offer no protection

I pray to my most empty beholder-

protect me from what I want,

and save me from my need

when I crave the kind

of solitude that only ever came

from the feeling of a fleeting love

I lose me,

in another sweaty song

of false comfort in another.

the heat wanes,

and I see myself

as I am

alone

and further down

a road of my own making

holding, tenderly,

these same ideals-

and my swinging, shining, could-bes

boys with twinkling eyes

of bright white light

in pools of dark, wet wonder

voices stained red

with ashes heaving

love sung loudly, and too soon

shimmering words

of sweet entanglements,

spoken softly- vulnerable and wide

characters unknown

with fuller thought and stood graces

all lay unreal,

beneath me and bolstered

I find ground to fall on-

golden, bleached, and chained

with dew drop skin

I stick to

nervous glances that quietly ask

for approval to be loved-

I surrender,

to the perfect pieces

of myself, in another

locked lips. spinning-

hot, held, and blue

NEW   SKIN,   I'M   UNFOLDING

back in my body,

I don't recognize the shape-

new skin, I'm unfolding

shedding, and pulling

writing in me

on my walls

of bloodied and pink skin,

scratches where

reverse I write,

echos from within.

I pick off scabs

so I can watch

the ways that I will heal-

I like to see

my skin unmasked,

and feel myself as real

VERSIONS   OF   MYSELF   WHISPER

SOFTLY   DIFFERENT   STORIES

when I sit

and I lie

with greatness, beasts, and vain imaginations-

the objects in my mirrors

appear to be bigger,

and hold

like unturned stones

I toe invincibility,

smiling

holding hands with thinning air,

and quickly shifting states

of mine heavy, strong, and worn out breeze

slipping through fingers fine

lifting waves of thunders

down and up, in cracks in time

my mind's edges fall away

between unspoken vulnerabilities

and beings in dissociation,

like reflections of who I am

holding unanswers

and small deaths

that keep

forming and reforming

in arguments for self-preservation

I make room for ache

into rebirth, becoming-

shifting pieces, pretending

expectations of me-

heavy and churning-

lay fractured,

fluid, and nameless

N A M E L E S S

I pull names in ink,

like swords in stone

or stuck rough rope

on through calloused hands,

begrudging and heavy

across lines

for the fifth time-

Brian- Emily- Katherine- Gregory- Ignacious-

looping cursive letters

that don't look quite right;

like hieroglyphs,

in the dawn of digitality

I reap, eat-

are you man enough?

I repeat,

are you good?

my gift is my warmth-

I hope you remember me like this.

glass skin, shifting.

hot to touch.

THE MYTH OF ME

I am not left without scars

that did not bloom and blossom

across the skin of Me,

slowly and shimmery,

in a white clean flight of flame

sparked by my own hand

and kindled by complacency

in my lonely and regardless

disrespect for the power

of changing fates

wished upon through tears

and selfish vanities,

spurred on by

the myth of me

that I don't speak to,

except to stand in awe of

or run from

in windy grand wonder

to the beat

of choirs of great kings

who roll through me

in waves,

on in my seismic line,

where I can sometimes feel

a deeper thunder

that tickles me with fear

and moves me out of place

until I am bending

under the weight

of this blending

and realize that I have drifted

much too far from shores

where I could sit

and slowly sunder

instead of spinning

where I could drown

under threat

of these thoughts

that do leave an echo

and things

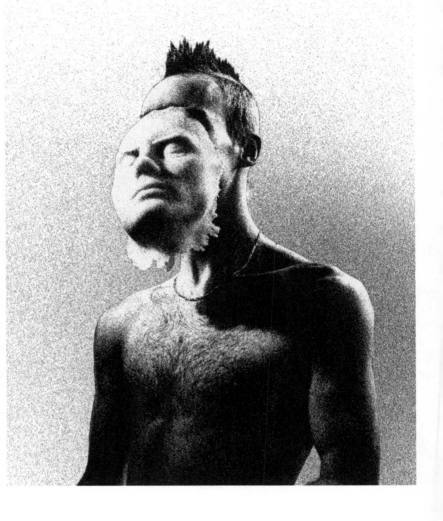

that feel better broken.

I hold it

and tell it

that we will learn to float

through that heavy shiver

and on,

to my coveted walls

of wet new wonder

THIS IS A DECLARATION OF LOVE

feet on fire,

my legs up in the air

I see you like you might be

afraid, and beautiful, and fair-

there was howling in the wind

as I watched the mountains fall

awash in the golden glowing might

of days that feel too tall

I put my roots in other people,

I don't have ground my own

crack me open, dump me out

just don't leave me alone

7 foot 2, I stand, over you

but no one ever made me feel so small

I hope im like my mother

proud of me, and kind, and tall

my heart is in the hardwood

that creaks with every step

some mistakes are too heavy to hold

this, I can accept-

lying in the grass, blue skies, sweet eyes,

I'll take you all-

there is nothing to remember.

I answer when you call

IN   THE   CORNER   OF   YOUR   EYE

you're still peeling that orange

and we like it upside down

it's purple and you're purple too

I see you, soft and new

I think I see you for the first time

and I can't stop looking

and I can't stop spitting, too

your neck is red

where I tried to bite it

and your orange

in pieces on the floor

you're sticky but I hold your hand

we're both sticky now

and it makes you start to cry

I'm warm

and it's beautiful

it feels like a goodbye

but you don't let go this time

and this time, neither do I

I ask you

are you falling?

you're not tired

you're just yawning

I hold you close inside of me

like I am your mother

you laugh in there

where I am warm

where I am most your lover

my voice is not mine -

it's calm and floats and shines

are you doing okay in there?

other than shining

I feel you, bent and warn

I'm stuck in me

I'm stuck on you

in you, I feel warm

THIS   POSSESSED   FLESH

I don't know why I stay

a snail in the crack of your bark

like a little corpse I lay

and roll about this mark

red never looked so bloody

I just might dance on my toes

we both might be muddy

but I don't pretend to know

plucking your fiddle

the pansys all cry

you hold me in my middle-

like I've seen few devotions fly

there's nothing in my hand

48, black tar, something like an itch

the wall leans from the land

like lines I cannot match

there's blackened fruit and fallen seeds,

to peel back your mystery

but all my swarming creature needs

fear your written history

in the pity of the dark

you bent me over the night,

ass out in the marching wind, stark

and came on my primal fright

I think with sight

that I'll never be the same

as I sit and fit and write

and my walls go up in flame

in my view,

all things have a place.

I choke on words and swallow you,

heart beat in my face.

IN   A   HEAVY   SHIVER

it's dark out now

bring in the chairs

the skin is on the floor

skins, I feel you

shifting quickly

so opens up the door

I ask me, and

I ask me, and

I say that I will listen

you feel higher

and I feel smaller

I think I feel me glisten

don't look at me

looking at me

I see you looking at you

I've never seen

myself like this,

like how it might be true

who I, am I

who then is she

who am I, I, can see

shedding person

in the mirror

give birth to you,

to me

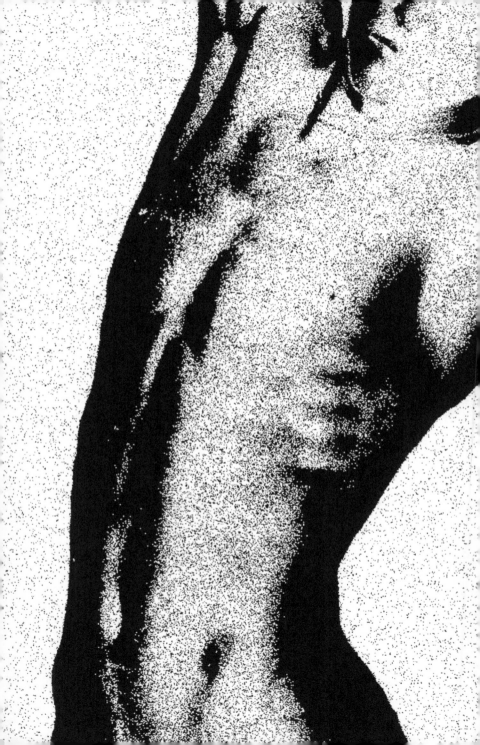

I   TAKE   MANY   SHAPES

wobbling, taller, free-er
and tightly all still mine -

humbly, faltered, green
broken, new, and unseen -

alive, and flying, brightly
taught, uglier (rightly) -

sorry sadness, reborn
glowing and finally unworn -

taken, distraught, and floating
distant, climbing, loading -

I am me,
stitched from vast we's
that I took long
and down the line

W   I   T   N   E   S   S

yesterday, I came to

and asked my heart

one last shock

feared,

surprise rippled audibly

and my mind shakes

in the in-between

her name was hesitation,

his new sensitivity- love

humbled by confirmation

of how much I need

I lean in-

looking out over this vast trust

I bring back together

me, as I am acceptable

sitting in solitude

with infinite versions of myself,

I stand on the corpses

of who I have been-

and my future forms keep me

we are all being watched

from the future, inside

by the people

that we come to be-

alive and frozen

in memory.

at the crossroads

of every one

that I could come to be,

I let my selves, see.

the self, as ever-changing and unknown

is my most pure perspective

and in my acceptance of myself

as many and endless and undefined

there is an ever-expanding line

a drunk and discordant choir,

of singing ghosts

within my mind

congruent and contradictory-

multiplicity feels free

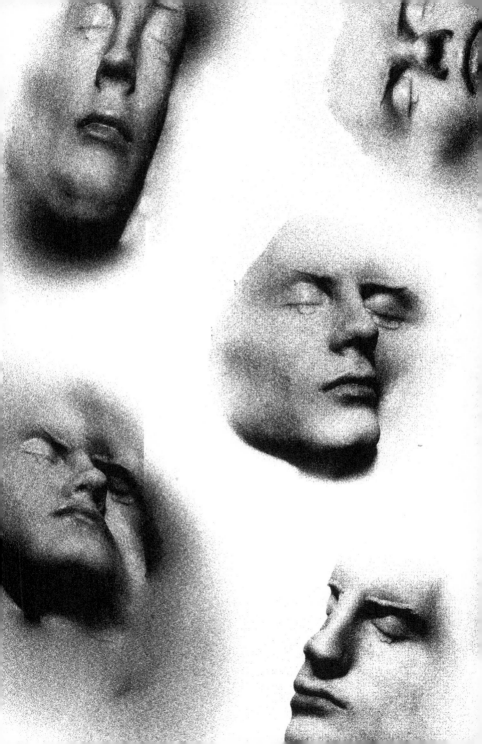

AUGUR EDITIONS

9 780578 871776